God's BIG ADVENTURE

Covenant & Kingdom for Kids

vol. 1

by Jason Byerly

3DM Publishing

God's Big Adventure, Volume 1
© Copyright 2015 by 3DM
written by Jason Byerly

Published by 3DM Publishing

Design: Blake Berg, Becky Rabb
Edited by: Robert Neely

ISBN: 978-0-9965300-0-2

3DM Publishing
3dmpublishing.com

CONTENTS

the
BEST
Story Ever!

What's your **favorite** story? That's a hard question to answer because we live in a world surrounded by so many amazing stories. Think about it. From the time you were a baby, you've been blasted with zillions of stories from books to movies, TV shows, comic books, and even video games and songs.

They all tell stories.

If you had to pick just one story—one ultimate, awesome, mind-blowing story—to be your all-time favorite, what would it be?

That's a tough choice. Or is it?

How about if I told you that one story is so much bigger, so much better, and so much more exciting than any other that it blows all the other stories right out of the water?

And the coolest part is that it's totally, 100 percent true. Wait, it gets better.

What if I told you that this fantastic, true story wasn't just a story to watch or to read? It's a story that you actually get to live. That's right. You don't just imagine it. You get to experience it yourself.

This ultimate, thrill-a-minute adventure story is God's story, and it can be your story, too.

Believe it or not, I'm talking about the Bible, and in its pages, God is inviting you to live an adventure unlike any other.

In this adventure, you will discover that the all-powerful King of Creation loves you like a perfect Dad, but this cosmic Dad also has a big job for you. He's building a kingdom, and you get to help.

The Bible is the story of God sharing His love and His adventure with His people.

Throughout this story, you're going to see those things come up again and again and again. We call it covenant and kingdom. Covenant is God's love story. Kingdom is His adventure story.

There's also a villain in God's story, and so that means there's battle, plenty of exciting battle.

Over the next few chapters, let's take a look at the love story, the adventure story, and where the battle began.

In each part of the story, we'll . . .

①

LOOK
UP!

to see what God
has to say.

③

LOOK
OUT!

to see how we can take
the story to people who
are outside God's family.

②

LOOK
IN!

to see how to live out
the story with faith-filled
friends.

What are you waiting for? Turn the
page, and let your adventure begin!

BFFs

Read: 1 John 4:7-9

Remember: How great is the love the Father has given us so freely! Now we can be called children of God. And that's what we really are!
– 1 John 3:1 (NIrV)

Where do you start the coolest story of all time? With the coolest character of all time! God. The Bible tells us many things about God. He is big, powerful, holy, amazing, and perfect.

God has so much power He could play ping-pong with planets, kickball with comets, and soccer with the sun. If you had that much power, what would you do with it? Create a roller-coaster the size of the Milky Way? Make yourself a million video games? Build a castle made of ice-cream and eat your way out of it?

IF *YOU* HAD THAT MUCH POWER, WHAT WOULD *YOU* DO WITH IT?

Most of us would probably use that kind of power in a selfish way, but not God. See, of all the incredible things we know about God, the most awesome thing is that God is love. Love is never selfish.

God used His power to create a planet full of people just to love. This all-powerful, all-knowing, all-everything God made ordinary people like you and me to be a part of His family. He wants to be our Dad in heaven and the best friend we've ever had.

What words would you use to describe the perfect friend? Loyal? Generous? Understanding? Protective? Fun? Kind?

Well, guess what? God is all that and more!

God wants to have a special relationship with you that's better than anything else. The Bible calls it a covenant. That's a fancy word that means you and God can become closer than close. God shares all of His stuff with you, and you share all of your stuff with God (which is a great deal, because God has way more stuff than us). It means God protects us and gives us everything we need.

It also means He never gives up on us. He is a faithful friend no matter where we go or what kind of mistakes we make.

This week, remember that even when you don't feel special, you'll always be special to God. He wants you to be a part of His royal family. That is where your true adventure begins.

LOOK UP! Take a sheet of paper and brainstorm as many amazing things about God that you can think of. Then flip the sheet over, and think of all the amazing things God would say that He loves about you. Remember, God is crazy about you!

LOOK IN! Being a part of God's family means we have lots of brothers and sisters to love, too. God wants us to share His love with others who are following Jesus. How can you be a faithful friend to another Jesus follower this week?

LOOK OUT! Just like God invited us into His family, He wants us to invite others into our family who don't know Him yet. Your mission today is to find one way to show kindness to someone you know who doesn't know Jesus.

God, thank you that you love me, that you want to be my friend and my perfect Dad. Help me to remember that you're with me, no matter where I go or what I do. Amen.

Royally Awesome

Read: Psalm 47:6-8

Remember: Who is this King of glory? The Lord strong and mighty, the Lord mighty in battle.
— Psalm 24:8 (NIV)

God's story isn't just a story about our friendship with God. It's also about joining God on an adventure. The Bible says God is on a mission. He's in a battle. He's building a kingdom, and we get to be part of the action.

Have you ever played a game of checkers and made it to the other side of the board? What happens? You yell, "King me!" or "Crown me!" Suddenly, your ordinary old checker turns into a super-checker able to do all kinds of cool things. The same thing happens when we become friends with God. When we are a part of God's royal family, the King crowns us with authority and power to do His work in the world.

That's when incredible things start to happen.

Think of authority like a police officer's badge. A police officer's badge shows people that he or she is authorized by the government to uphold the law. In the same way, God gives you a badge of authority that shows that you have His permission to act for Him. It's not a badge that anyone can actually see. But it's still real. You are authorized to stand in for the King. That means you can do good things in God's name wherever you go.

WHAT'S SOMETHING GOOD THAT YOU CAN DO?

Not only does God give you the authority to do good stuff, but He also gives you the power to do it. If authority is like a badge, then God's power is like a weapon. It's the power to do amazing things for God. Of course, the only one this weapon hurts is the devil, but we'll get to that later.

For now, you just need to know that your heavenly Dad, who loves you, has a big job for you to do. Your job is to bring good stuff from heaven to earth. You do that by living like Jesus and by letting God's light shine in every good thing you do.

LOOK UP! Draw the coolest crown you can and put it somewhere to remind you that you get to show people the King by the way you live.

LOOK IN! All of us need encouragement when we're on an adventure with God. How can you encourage your faith-filled friends to do good things this week? Who can you pray for?

LOOK OUT! Living God's adventure means reaching out to people who don't yet know God. It means sharing God's love and encouragement. An easy way to do this is to make someone a card and let them know you're thinking about them. Who can you encourage with a card today?

God, thanks for inviting me to join your adventure. Help me to copy Jesus and show people what you're like by the way I live. Amen!

The Battle is On

Read: Ephesians 6:10-18

Remember: Don't let evil overcome you.
Overcome evil by doing good.
— Romans 12:21 (NIrV)

Who's the worst movie villain you can think of? What makes them so bad? Sometimes, villains in the movies can be funny or even kind of entertaining. However, in real life, there's only one villain, and there's nothing funny or entertaining about him at all. His name's Satan, and he can't stand God or any of God's kids. Why? He's got a major case of jealousy.

Here's what happened. A long time ago, Satan was an angel in heaven, and his job, just like that of all the other angels, was to worship God. The only problem was somewhere along the way Satan thought it would be better if everyone worshipped him. He had a serious ego problem.

WHO'S THE WORST VILLAIN THAT *YOU* CAN THINK OF?

Then, in what seems like a fairly boneheaded move, he tried to knock God off His throne. It was an epic fail. God totally smoked Satan. No surprise there. Angels may look impressive to us, but compared to God, they're nothing. Satan never stood a chance.

God kicked Satan out of heaven along with a bunch of angels who followed him. Since he can't hurt God, Satan has been trying to mess with God by leading God's kids away from God and making the world a bad place.

Satan will do anything to break up the covenant and kingdom that God wants to give His kids. Satan's pretty good at it, too. In a couple of chapters, we'll see how he tricked the first people into turning their backs on God and bringing a curse on the entire planet.

Bummer, huh?

However, just when Satan thought he was scoring major points, along came Jesus! Jesus, the King of Kings, came to earth, broke the curse of sin, and sent the devil packing. When Jesus died on the cross and rose from the dead, he beat the devil and won the war.

One day, Jesus will return to earth and put an end to Satan once and for all, but for now, Satan is still hanging around, beaten, but trying to make life miserable for God's kids.

That's okay. With God's power, we'll make life even more miserable for Satan. Remember, we have the authority of God's badge, and we have the weapon of God's power. It's our job to use that power to bring good stuff into the world and destroy the work of the devil.

We may be in a battle, but it has already been won.

LOOK UP! How many words can you think of that describe God's power (big, awesome, unstoppable, etc)? Can you come up with one for every letter of the alphabet?

LOOK IN! As God's family, we never have to face the enemy alone. We can pray for each other, encourage each other, and remind each other what's right and wrong. Which one of your faith-filled friends can you help in their fight against evil this week?

LOOK OUT! Pray for God to show you one bad thing in the world that you can make better by doing some good. Maybe it's someone who's sad who needs a friend or someone hungry who needs some food or someone who just needs to know that Jesus loves them.

God, thank you that I don't have to be afraid of Satan. Thank you that your power protects me. Please use me this week to overcome evil with good in my school, in my home, and in my world. Amen.

The Very First Birthday

Read: Genesis 2:4-7

Remember: How you made me is amazing and wonderful. I praise you for that.
– Psalm 139:14 (NIrV)

Have you ever felt lonely, sad, or afraid? Have you ever felt like you needed something you didn't have to make you happy?

Of course, you have. There's a reason for that. It's because all people were made to live in a super-close friendship with God. When we're not close to God, we miss Him, even if we don't realize it.

HAVE YOU EVER FELT LONELY, SAD, OR AFRAID?

Way back at the beginning of time, right after God made the awesome universe and everything in it, He made the very first people. Here's how it happened.

God reached down, scooped up some clay from the earth, and began to shape His special creation. God mashed and molded and stretched the clay with His fingers until He got it just the way He wanted it. Of all the wonderful things God had made, this was His greatest masterpiece!

Then, came the best part. God gave the new man life. The clay turned to skin. The eyes opened, and Adam woke up for the very first time. It was the first birthday ever!

Next, God made a woman named Eve to be Adam's partner. Because they had been made by God, they both had the fingerprints of God all over them. And so do you!

When you make something with clay, you leave a handprint on it. In the same way, God has left His impression on you. You're made in

God's image just like Adam and Eve were.

 That means that not only are you God's work of art, and not only are you made to represent God to the world, but you also are made to always be close with God. He wants to fill up your heart with His love.

LOOK UP! Make your own special creation today with some modeling dough or clay. Think about how God shaped you in a special way to be His friend.

LOOK IN! God knew it wasn't good for people to be alone all the time. That's why He gave Adam a partner. Who are the faith- filled friends God has given you to do life with? Tell them how thankful you are for them today.

LOOK OUT! Every person you meet is God's special creation. Every person matters to God. Show someone outside of God's family how special they are to God by showing them they are special to you. Invite them to play or hang out and treat them like royalty.

God, thank you for making me special. Please come and fill up my heart today with your love. Remind me how special I am to you even when I don't feel like it. Amen!

Charging Your Batteries

Read: Genesis 2:1-3

Remember: By the seventh day God had finished the work he had been doing; so on the seventh day he rested from all his work.
– Genesis 2:2.

Throughout God's big story, we'll take a look at some simple shapes that will help us to think about ways we can take part in God's story too.

Do you know what this shape is? It's a semi-circle. Can you find anything in your house that's this shape?

This semi-circle will remind us of how God wants us to charge up our batteries before we go adventuring with him.

CAN YOU FIND ANYTHING IN YOUR HOUSE THAT'S THIS SHAPE?

REST ← → **WORK**

That arrow kind of looks like a swing going back and forth. One side of the swing is rest. The other side is work.

God always wants us to start with rest. Rest our bodies. Rest our brains. Rest our hearts. That way we have plenty of energy to go out and do big stuff with him.

After we do stuff—do some work—we rest some more to keep from crashing. Rest. Work. Rest. Work. Back and forth. Back and forth.

When God made Adam and Eve, I bet they were ready to get to work. But guess what God had them do first? Rest! Sounds crazy, right? Why would they need to rest before they'd even done anything?

Because God loved them. He wanted to spend time with them. He feels the same way about you. Spending time with God is more important than any work we could ever do for God.

Of course God does want us to do good things. He wants us to work. He just knows that we need to charge up our batteries before we go take action.

LOOK UP! God loves to spend time with you. He loves to fill you up with his strength and power. Pick a regular time and place to hang out with God every day.

LOOK IN! Does your family spend more time resting or working? Do you have time to hang out and have fun, or are you always rushing to the next thing? Do you need to plan some down time together? What could your down time look like?

LOOK OUT! Once you are rested, God has big things for you to do with his power to change the world. Who can you help? What can you do to share God's love?

God, please teach me how to rest and recharge. Please fill me up so I can do big things with you. Amen.

A Gigantic Job

Read: Genesis 2:15-20

Remember: The LORD God put the man in the Garden of Eden. He put him there to work its ground and to take care of it.
— Genesis 2:15 (NIrV)

Have you ever had an important job to do? Maybe it was to watch your baby sister, deliver a message to someone, or be a special helper at school? How did it make you feel to have such a big responsibility?

When God created Adam and Eve, He gave them a big responsibility, too. Their job was to take care of the amazing things God had made. God let them rule over His kingdom in the Garden of Eden and stand in for Him.

They were His representatives. They means they got to do special jobs for God.

Adam even got to name all of the animals. Just imagine that. A brown furry thing comes swinging out of the trees, and Adam says, "Let's call it a monkey!" From then on, it was a monkey. Pretty cool, huh?

WHAT NAME WOULD YOU GIVE TO A MONKEY?

But as cool as it was, it was also a big responsibility. Taking care of God's kingdom means doing things God's way. With a big relationship comes a big responsibility. God gave Adam and Eve this huge kingdom job because He loved them so much.

He still does the same thing today. Because God loves us, we get to represent God wherever we go—at home, school, our neighborhood, or anywhere else. We also get to help take care of God's creation. That includes the way we treat other people. When we live God's way by showing love and kindness, we help bring God's kingdom to earth.

LOOK UP! Get outside and take a walk. What are the coolest things you see that God made? Tell Him how awesome they are.

LOOK IN! For a big job we need lots of help. God gives us other believers to help us take care of His creation and to build His kingdom. Who is one person who helps you to follow God and do good things?

LOOK OUT! We all have a responsibility to show people what God is like. We do that by the things we say and the things we do. Imagine someone who didn't know anything about God. What would they think about God just by looking at how you treat them? What is one thing you could do differently to give people a better picture of God's love?

God, thank you for letting me care for your creation. Please help me to bring your kingdom wherever I go by doing things your way. Amen.

Independence Day

Read: Genesis 3:1-10

Remember: Teach me how to live as you have promised. Don't let any sin be my master.
— Psalm 119:133 (NIrV)

It's fun to be able to do things on your own, isn't it? Think about the first time you tied your own shoe or learned to swim or ride a bike. It feels great to be able to do this stuff without the help of a grown-up. That's called independence, and it's a good thing.

However, there's another kind of independence that's not so good. It's when we think we can do life without God. That leads to all kinds of trouble. God made us to depend on Him for everything we need, especially when we're trying to make a wise choice.

Sometimes, though, we don't listen to God. Sometimes, we think we don't need Him. That's a big mistake and always messes up the good things God wants to give us.

Take Adam and Eve, for instance. They had it made. They had a special friendship with God and got to rule God's world as long as they listened to God. He gave them tons of freedom. In fact, they had only one rule in the whole world. Can you imagine having only one rule?

God told them they could eat the delicious food from every tree in Eden except for one. He told them not to eat from it or they would die. God gave them this rule to protect them.

HAVE YOU EVER BEEN TEMPTED TO DO THINGS YOUR OWN WAY?

But they didn't listen. They didn't trust God. Instead, they listened to God's enemy, who was disguised as a snake. Satan didn't make them do anything. He just lied to them, and they chose to believe him and disobey God.

Adam and Even did things their own way and ruined everything. By disobeying God, they brought a curse on the planet. Sickness, sadness, and sin entered the world that day.

And Adam and Eve? They couldn't live in the perfect garden anymore. They couldn't rule God's world anymore. So Satan took over in their place.

Worst of all, they couldn't live in that perfect friendship with God.

How about you? When have you been tempted to do things your way instead of God's way? Do you depend on God to help you make wise choices? What happens when you don't?

LOOK UP!

Write down one area where you're tempted to do things your way instead of God's way. Ask God to help you depend on Him this week to do the right thing.

LOOK IN!

We need faith-filled friends to remind us to do things God's way. We can pray for each other and encourage each other to keep doing what's right. We can also warn each other of danger when we get close to sin. Is there someone you need to pray for, encourage, or warn today?

LOOK OUT!

Adam and Eve messed up the whole world when they chose to sin. We can begin to fix the world by doing things God's way instead. One way you can do that is by serving. Is there someone on your street or at your school you can help today?

God, thank you for always showing me the right thing to do, and for loving me even when I blow it. Help me to listen to you, trust you and depend on you this week. Amen!

Bad News, Good News

Read: Genesis 3:21-24

Remember: He does not treat us as our sins
deserve.
— Psalm 103:10 (NIV)

What is the grossest food you can imagine? I'm talking about food so disgusting it would make you lose your lunch. Spinach? Sauerkraut? Liver?

Whatever it is for you, imagine how you would feel if someone dumped it all over your favorite dessert.

WHAT'S THE GROSSEST FOOD YOU CAN IMAGINE?

Ugh! The dessert would be ruined. It doesn't mean you don't love the dessert. It doesn't mean you don't want the dessert. It's just that the gross food would make it too nasty to have near you. You might even push it away.

That's kind of how God feels about sin. It grosses Him out. God is perfect, what the Bible calls holy. It means God has no sin at all. Never has. Never will. God can't stand sin. He pushes sin away because it's so disgusting to Him.

That's why when Adam and Eve sinned by eating the fruit, God pushed them away, too. He kicked them out of the Garden of Eden and put angel guards at the entrance to make sure they didn't return. It didn't mean God didn't love them. It didn't even mean He didn't want them. It's just that now they had a sin problem, and God had to push away the sin.

Because God is holy, He had to push Adam and Eve away. The good news is that God's love is bigger than that. Did you notice in the story how kind God was to Adam and Eve even though they'd blown it? He made them clothes. He provided what they needed because he loved them.

God was already putting His plan into action that would bring people back to that perfect friendship with Him. He would someday send Jesus to take away sin so that no one would ever have to be pushed away from God again. (That part comes later.)

The great news that you can remember today is that no matter what you've done, God still loves you. He still wants to be your Dad in heaven, and He still wants you to join His adventure.

LOOK UP! Every time you see something gross this week, let it remind you of how God feels about sin and thank God for wiping your sin away.

LOOK IN! Friends who follow Jesus sometimes make bad choices and hurt each other's feelings or get into fights. God wants us to forgive each other just like He forgives us. Is there anyone you need to forgive?

LOOK OUT! Sometimes people outside God's family make bad choices, too, but God still wants us to love them. That doesn't mean we approve of their choices or follow their example. It does mean we find ways to love them and serve them no matter what they've done.

God, thanks for loving me even though I do wrong things. Thank you for still wanting to be my Dad in heaven and do great things through me. Amen!

The Big, Wet Do-Over

Read: Genesis 6:5-9

Remember: God, create a pure heart in me.
Give me a new spirit that is
faithful to you.
– Psalm 56:10 (NIrV)

Have you ever been playing a game and messed up so badly that you asked for a "do-over"? A do-over is when you want a second chance to get it right. Not long after Adam and Eve left the Garden of Eden, God was ready for a do-over with the entire earth. It wasn't because God had messed up. It was because His people had messed up and had become so bad.

You would think that Adam and Eve's kids and grandkids would have learned from Adam and Eve's mistake. But they didn't.

After Adam and Eve were kicked out of Eden, people's behavior just went from bad to worse. In the days after Adam and Eve, the Bible says that people did evil things all the time.

It got so bad that God finally said, "Enough! It's time for a do-over. I'm starting from scratch!" He didn't use those exact words, but that's what He meant. God had decided to flood the world to clean away all the bad stuff and all the bad people. That was pretty much everybody, except for one guy and his family.

The man's name was Noah. Unlike most people in those days, Noah was friends with God. Noah wasn't perfect, but he understood the whole relationship and responsibility thing. Noah hung out with God, and he did everything God told him to do.

God told Noah to build a huge boat and get ready for all the animals God would send Noah's way. Long story short, God super-soaked the planet and destroyed all the evil people. Sounds kind of harsh, right? Remember, God is the holy King who can't stand sin. Something had to be done.

Thankfully, God is also a loving dad so He saved Noah and his family. After the flood, God made a promise that He would never flood the earth like that again no matter how bad it got. He put a special rainbow in the sky to remind people of His promise of mercy.

WHAT WOULD YOU LIKE TO DO OVER?

With that promise, God made the first move to reach out to His kids to fix the mess they had started in the Garden of Eden. Eventually, God's Son Jesus would come and take care of sin once and for all. He would make it possible for all of our hearts to be flooded with his love and washed clean.

Today, God promises that no matter how much we blow it, when we turn to Jesus, we can have all the do-overs we need as we learn to follow Him.

LOOK UP! Have a grown-up help you find instructions on the Internet for making a paper boat. Write a prayer on the paper you use to make the boat and thank God for do-overs.

LOOK IN! Sometimes we need a do-over with our friends. We mess up our friendship by fighting, being selfish, or saying mean things. Do you need to say "I'm sorry" to anyone today?

LOOK OUT! The world is full of people who don't know Jesus and need a do-over in life. You can show them God's love by being their friend even if no one else will.

God, thank you for saving Noah and his family. Thank you for saving me, too, through Jesus. Thank you for giving me do-overs as you make me more like Jesus. Amen.

Action Heroes

Read: Genesis 6:9-18

Remember: Noah did everything just as God commanded him.
— Genesis 6:22

Here's another simple shape to help us play our part in God's story.

What shape is this? What are some circle-shaped things you see every day in your house or at school?

This circle is going to help us understand how to listen to God and do what he says. God still speaks to people every day, but not everyone listens to him.

Some other people actually do listen to God. They just don't do what God tells them.

You know what made Noah different than everyone around him? He did **both**. He heard God's voice, and he took action! Because Noah did these two things, he got to be a part of an amazing adventure, and he saved his family and a whole bunch of animals along the way.

By listening to God and doing what he says, you can be an action hero just like Noah.

This circle is like a treasure map we follow to discover God's surprises. The circle is the path that helps us to hear from God and do what he says. And that always leads us to a big adventure.

Here's how it works:

Kairos Moment:

This is when God breaks into your day with something to say.

Kairos

X

Step 1: OBSERVE
You say "Whoa! That's God talking!"

Step 2: REFLECT
You say, "Hmm, wonder what he's trying to tell me?"

Step 3: DISCUSS
You talk about it with someone else who loves God. Ask them what they think God is saying. What does he want you to know or do?

Step 4: PLAN
Make a plan, Stan. Ask yourself, "How am I going to put what God's saying into action? What's my plan?"

Step 5: ACCOUNT
It's time to get a buddy. Find a faith-filled friend who can pray for you and your plan. Make sure they ask you about it later to see how it went.

Act — Observe

Account — Reflect

Plan — Discuss

Believe : Repent

Step 6: ACT
Just do it! Put the plan to work, and watch God do something awesome with it!

That's it. Just follow the circle to listen to God and do what he says. Along the way, you'll discover the cool surprises and adventure God has planned just for you.

 LOOK **UP!** — What's God saying to you today? Is there a certain Bible verse you keep thinking about? Or maybe something you feel like God wants you to do? Where is God getting your attention?

LOOK **IN!** — Who are some people you can talk to about whatever it is God might be saying?

LOOK **OUT!** — Who are people God might be sending you to help today?

God, thanks for talking to me. Please help me to learn to hear your voice and help me to have the courage to do whatever you tell me to do. Amen.

The Babbling Builders

Read: Genesis 11:1-9

Remember: If the LORD doesn't build a house, the work of its builders is useless.
– Psalm 127:1 (NIrV)

Have you ever known someone who thought they were a big deal just because they could do big things? Whether it's a kid who's athletic or smart, fashionable or funny, people who are full of pride can be frustrating. Especially to God.

In the next part of God's story, there are some people who thought they were a big deal but were really just a bunch of show-offs.

Long after Noah's family came out of the ark, the earth began to fill up with people again. But these people were still separated from God.

Just like everyone since Adam and Eve, they felt the big empty hole in their hearts that could only be filled by their Dad in heaven. Since they didn't have God, they tried to fill up that hole by doing something big.

"Then they said, 'Come. Let's build a city for ourselves. Let's build a tower that reaches to the sky.'" (Genesis 11:4 NIrV)

In those days, people thought that God lived just above the sky. If they could build a tower big enough to break through the clouds, they thought maybe they could get to God.

They didn't really care about God. They were just full of themselves and wanted everyone to see how awesome they were by building this big tower. They were full of the worst kind of pride.

Their big accomplishment made them think they didn't need God. They thought if they could build this tower they could do anything on their own. When God saw this, he knew he had to put a stop to it, because life apart from God is the worst thing ever. God knew if the people kept working together, they would just run farther and farther away from his love.

God came down and mixed up their languages so that no one could understand each other. After that, they didn't get a whole lot done. Eventually, they gave up building the tower and went and lived in different countries. Pride turned their big accomplishment into a big flop.

This week, you're probably not going to try to build a gigantic tower to heaven, but you might be tempted to show off and brag. You might be tempted to think that the big things you do make you a big deal.

HAVE YOU EVER THOUGHT YOU WERE A BIG DEAL AND DIDN'T NEED GOD?

When that happens, remember that you're already a big deal because you're loved by a big God. You're God's kid. It's great to do big things and be good at stuff, but all of this stuff without a friendship with God doesn't mean a thing.

LOOK UP! Build the biggest tower you can out of blocks, pillows or something else. Once you make it as big as you can, knock it down to remind yourself that without God our biggest accomplishments don't mean a thing.

LOOK IN! Pride and bragging can get in the way of being a good friend. The next time you're tempted to brag to your friends, choose to celebrate someone else instead. Brag about your friends instead of yourself.

LOOK OUT! At the tower of Babel, people were separated because they spoke different languages. Now, though, Jesus' love brings people together no matter how different they are. Do you know anyone who is from another country or speaks a different language? Invite them over to play or hang out this week.

God, thanks for giving me the ability to do big things, but help me to remember that having you as my Dad is the biggest thing of all. Amen!

Go Time

Read: Genesis 12:1-5

Remember: Trust in the Lord with all your heart. Do not depend on your own understanding. In all your ways remember him. Then he will make your paths smooth and straight.
— Proverbs 3:5-6 (NIrV)

One of the hardest things about being a kid is that you have to do new stuff or go to new places all the time. You have your first day at a new school, first night away from home, first trip to the dentist and on and on it goes. Sometimes you get to take your friends or family along for the ride, but other times you might not. You might feel all alone.

There's a guy in the Bible named Abram who knew exactly how you feel. At the beginning of Abram's story he lived in a place called Ur.

Life was pretty good in Ur. Abram grew up there and knew his way around. He knew where to find the best cheeseburgers and laser tag and the coolest places to ride his bike. Okay, so maybe he didn't have that stuff, but Ur was comfy and familiar, and Abram could have been happy there forever.

He had plenty of servants and money and even a sweet wife named Sarai. But God had something even more awesome in store.

Out of the blue God said to Abram, "Leave your country and your people. Leave your father's family. Go to the land I will show you." (Genesis 12:1 NIrV)

In other words, God was saying, "Pack up all of your stuff and let's hit the road."

Just imagine if God told you to pack up all of your stuff and leave your house. Abram had to leave behind his friends, most of his family and everything he'd ever known.

He didn't even know where he was going. God just said, "Get moving and I'll tell you where it is when you get there."

Here's the craziest part. Abram actually did it! He got his wife Sarai, his nephew Lot and all his stuff and they set out for a brand new land called Canaan.

Think of how Abram must have felt to just up and move to a brand new place he'd never been. It was probably scary. It was probably lonely. Abram probably even got homesick. So why did he do it?

He did it because he knew that God takes care of His kids. Yes, it was scary going to this strange new place. Yes, it was lonely. Yes, he got homesick. But Abram knew he wasn't going alone. God was going with him, and that made all the difference.

LOOK UP! Draw a picture of yourself of doing something new that might make you nervous. When you're done, draw God into the picture. Use this drawing to remember that God will be with you wherever you go.

LOOK IN! Do you have any friends who are doing something new this week? Pray for them and let them know you're cheering them on.

LOOK OUT! Do you know anyone who is new to your school, neighborhood or town? What's one thing you can do to help them feel at home in this new place?

God, thank you for leading me on new adventures. Help me to trust you to take care of me when I go to new places and try new things. Amen!

Just What You Need

Read: Genesis 15:1-4

Remember: Abram, do not be afraid. I am like a shield to you. I am your very great reward.
— Genesis 15:1 (NIrV)

If you had a pirate treasure chest like you see in the movies, what would you put inside it? Video games? A toy? A cell phone? Clothes? Food? What is your greatest treasure?

One day, God told Abram that Abram had a great treasure. It was God Himself. He said, "I am your shield, Abram, your very great reward." In other words, God was telling Abraham that He was everything Abraham would ever need.

Like a shield, God promised to protect Abram, and like a treasure chest, God promised to provide everything Abram needed. Why? Because He loved Abram, just like He loves you.

God wants to have a relationship with you. He wants you to be His kid. As a loving Dad, God wants to protect and provide for you every day.

Think about all the ways God protects you in your everyday life. He protects you from storms and bullies and bike wrecks and probably all kinds of things we don't even know about. Think of all the things He provides for you by giving you things like food and clothes and friends and people who love you.

This week, think about what you need most from God. Do you need Him to be your Protector and keep you safe from something? Or do you need Him to be your Provider and give you something you need?

WHAT DO *YOU* NEED MOST FROM GOD THIS WEEK?

Whatever you need this week, God already knows it, and since He is our Dad in heaven, we can trust Him to take care of us no matter what.

LOOK UP!

Take a piece of paper and draw a shield on one side and a treasure chest on the other. Decorate them and make them cool. On the shield, write down all the ways you see God protecting you. On the treasure chest, write down all the things that God provides for you in your life.

LOOK IN!

We can be a protector like God by praying for other believers. Which of your friends needs prayers of protection this week? Pray for your friends now.

LOOK OUT!

We can be a provider like God by meeting the needs of others. This is a great way to show God's love to people who don't know Him yet. Who has a need that you can help with this week?

God, you are a loving Dad. You are my shield and my great reward. Please protect me and give me what I need as I follow you. Help us to trust you like Abram did no matter where you lead us. Amen!

God's Out-of-This-World Promise

Read: Genesis 15:5-6

Remember: Abram believed the Lord. The Lord accepted Abram because he believed. So his faith made him right with the Lord.
— Genesis 15:6 (NIrV)

Has anyone ever made you a gigantic promise? Maybe your teacher promised an awesome party for your class at the end of the year, or your parents promised to take you on a really cool vacation. Did you believe that promise? How did you know it would come true?

Those are big promises. However, they're nothing compared to the huge promise God made to Abram.

At this point in the story, Abram was bummed out because he still didn't have any kids. That meant that when he died, all of his stuff would go to his servant. I'm sure Abram's servant was a nice enough guy, but Abram wanted a child of his own. He wanted someone to carry on the family name. He wanted a big family.

God's promise was even bigger than that.

One night, God took Abram outside and said, "Abram, look up at the sky. You see all those stars? Count them if you can." (Genesis 15:5 NIrV)

Have you ever tried to count the stars on a really dark night? It's impossible because there are gazillions of them.

HOW MANY STARS DO YOU THINK THERE ARE?

Abram was busy counting away when God said, "That's how many children you're going to have." Whoa! Promising one child would have been amazing, but gazillions? That just sounds crazy!

Now Abram had a big choice to make. Should he believe God's promise or not? Just because God said it, could Abram count on it coming true?

Abram believed. He chose to have something called faith. Faith is trusting that God will do what He said He would do. Faith is confidence in God.

Because Abram believed God, God had a special friendship with Abram. Not only did He eventually give Abram a son, but now anyone who trusts God like Abram did is called a child of Abram.

Think about how many people have trusted God over the years. A gazillion, right? All those people, including you and me, are part of Abram's family of faith. All of God's promises for Abram came true!

LOOK UP! Take time to listen to God today. Read the Bible. Talk to God. Remember, like Abram, you can always count on God's promises to come true.

LOOK IN! Since you are a kid of the King, people should be able to trust your promises, too. Do you always do what you say? Can your friends trust you to be faithful to your words?

LOOK OUT! God wants us to invite new people to join Abram's family of faith every day. Who are the people God has placed in your life you can show God's love today?

God, thank you for your promises. Help me to trust you like Abram did and to remember that all of your promises will come true. Amen.

Name Calling

Read: Genesis 17:1-5

Remember: But God chose you to be his people. You are royal priests. You are a holy nation. You are a people who belong to God.
– 1 Peter 2:9 (NIrV)

Has anyone ever called you a name? Maybe they made fun of you and said something that hurt your feelings. Maybe they called you slow or dumb or clumsy or something even worse. Even if they are not true, these things still make us feel bad. Sometimes, we start to believe the mean things people say about us.

On the other hand, think how you felt when someone said something good about you. Maybe they even gave you a nickname that made you feel special. Maybe they called you "Flash" because you're so fast or "Einstein" because you get good grades. Or better yet, maybe your nickname has nothing to do with what you do. A dad might call his daughter "Princess" or his son "Champ" just because he loves them.

In today's story, we discover that our Dad in heaven loves to give us special names, too. One day, God told Abram He was going to change his name to Abraham. Abram means "Exalted Father," but Abraham means "Father of Nations."

This new name reminded Abraham of God's big plans and promises for his life. Abraham wasn't going to be the father of just one kid. He was going to be the dad and grandpa of a whole nation of people who loved God—anyone who put their faith in God!

I don't know what mean names people may have called Abraham when he was younger, but God's name for him was the only one that mattered. What God said about Abraham actually came true!

WHAT ARE SOME NAMES PEOPLE HAVE CALLED *YOU*?

The same thing is true for you. People may call you all kinds of names in your life, but the only thing that really matters is what God says about you. God calls you "His Kid." God calls you "Loved." God calls you "Royalty." God calls you "Ambassador," someone who stands in for Him and does big world-changing stuff.

This week forget what other people say about you. Just listen to what God says about you. What God says about you is always true!

HELLO
my name is

LOOK UP! Get a sticky name tag or make one and write on it your favorite name that God calls you. Put it somewhere where it can remind you that what God says about you is the only thing that matters.

LOOK IN! Kids of the King need to remind each other how special they are to God. Write a note to one of your Christian friends and remind them that they are awesome and wonderful to God and you.

LOOK OUT! When you hear kids calling someone a mean name, stand up for them. Tell them something positive that you like about them instead.

God, what you say is always true. Please help me to remember this week the special names that you have for me. Help me never to believe mean things others may say about me, but that what you say is the only thing that counts. Amen!

Finally!

Read: Genesis 18:9-15

Remember: Every good and perfect gift is
from God.
— James 1:17 (NIrV)

Have you ever wanted something really bad but you had to wait for it for a long time? What was it? A Christmas or birthday present? Summer vacation? Maybe getting your first bike? It's hard to wait, isn't it? It seems like forever.

Abraham and Sarah had to wait a long, long time for God to come through on His promise. Abraham was 75 years old when God first promised him a son. He didn't just have to wait days or months or even a couple of years. He and Sarah waited twenty-five long years for God to give them what He had promised.

Then one day, totally out of the blue, God and a couple of angels showed up at Abraham's tent. God was walking with His people that day, just like He used to do back in the Garden of Eden.

God told Abraham that he and his wife Sarah were finally about to have a son, but when Sarah heard it, she laughed. She thought what God said sounded crazy.

However, a year later, Sarah was laughing with joy, because God's promise had finally come true. Abraham and Sarah had a brand-new baby son. This boy, Isaac, would be special because God would work through Isaac and his family to begin fixing the relationship with God that Adam and Eve had messed up in Eden.

One day, another special baby, the most special baby ever, would come from Isaac's family. Jesus. Jesus would come to bring us back into that covenant friendship with God once and for all.

See, God's best is always worth waiting for.

WHAT IS SOMETHING YOU HAD TO WAIT FOR?

You may end up waiting on all kinds of things from God. Maybe you're waiting for God to help you make a friend in a new school or deal with a bully. You could be waiting on God to show you the right thing to do in a tough situation or to give you the chance to talk to someone about Jesus.

Whatever it is, remember that you can always trust God to keep His promises and give you His very best.

LOOK UP! Get a grown-up to help you make cookies or another special treat that needs to be baked. Once it goes in the oven, sit and stare at it the whole time you're waiting for it to cook. After it's done, eat one of the treats and think about how the best things are worth waiting for.

LOOK IN! Waiting is always easier with a friend. Friends of God encourage each other as they wait on God. Do you have a friend who's waiting on God for something right now? Go hang out with them this week and remind them that God's best is always worth waiting for.

LOOK OUT! The world is full of people who don't know God who may be waiting for you to show up in their lives and bring them some hope. Who can you bring God's hope to this week? How can you do it?

God, thank you for your promises for me. Please help me to remember that your best is always worth waiting for. Amen.

One Tough Test

Read: Genesis 22:1-18

Remember: If you love me, you will obey
what I command.
– John 14:15 (NIrV)

If you could ask God to give you one thing, what would it be? A video game? A toy? A puppy? Maybe a baby brother or sister? Whatever it is, imagine that God actually gave it to you. Imagine that He heard your prayer and gave you exactly what you asked for. Your prayer was answered. Your wish was fulfilled. Your dream had finally come true.

Now, imagine that God asked for it back. Imagine if God told you that He wanted you to give up the very thing you had begged Him to give you. What if God told you to smash the video game, break the toy, or take the puppy to the dog pound? Would you do it? That would be pretty tough, wouldn't it?

That's exactly what happened to God's friend, Abraham. Abraham had waited twenty-five years for God to give him a son, and God finally did. Isaac wasn't just a normal kid to Abraham. Isaac was a reminder of God's special promise. Someday, God had said, Abraham would become the father of a big nation of people, and it would all start with Isaac.

Then one day, God tested Abraham to see how much Abraham really loved Him. He asked Abraham to give up the thing he loved more than anything else in the world—Isaac.

God said, "Take your son, you only son, whom you love—Isaac—and go to the region of Moriah. Sacrifice him there . . . on a mountain I will show you." (Genesis 22:2 NIV)

God didn't really want Abraham to hurt his son. God just wanted to see if Abraham loved God enough to give up everything for Him. Would Abraham trust God no matter what?

This was the hardest day of Abraham's life. He loved Isaac so much. How could he possibly give up his own son? Believe it or not, though, Abraham did it. Obeying God didn't make any sense, but Abraham knew that God is good, and he could trust God no matter what.

Abraham took Isaac up on a mountain, tied him up, and pulled out his knife. Abraham was just about to sacrifice Isaac when God said, "Abraham! Abraham! Do not lay a hand on the boy. Do not do anything to him!" (Genesis 22:11-12 NIV)

Now God knew Abraham wouldn't hold anything back from Him. Abraham really did love God more than anything else. Because Abraham didn't hold back from God, God didn't hold anything back from him. God blessed Abraham like crazy. Not only did Isaac have kids, but also his kids and their kids eventually became the nation of Israel.

Sometimes obeying God can be really hard. But when we remember we're God's kids and that God is a good Dad, it makes it a whole lot easier. We remember that God loves us, and we can trust Him. If He tells us to do something, it's always for good, even if it doesn't make sense.

LOOK UP! Pick your favorite toy or gadget and put it away for 24 hours. Every time you think about playing with it, think about how hard it must have been for Abraham to give up thing he loved most.

LOOK IN! Friends of God help each other obey God. When your friends are tempted to do what's wrong, do you encourage them to do what's right instead? Do your friends challenge you to make good choices?

LOOK OUT! By obeying God, we can show others what God is like and that He can be trusted. Are you setting a good example for your friends who don't know God? If not, where do you need God's help to change?

God, you're a good Dad. Please help me to remember that I can trust you no matter what. Help me to obey you because I'm your kid, and I love you. Amen.

God's Love Story

Read: Psalm 103:8-13

Remember: No, the Father himself loves you because you have loved me and believed that I came from God. – John 16:27

Do you recognize this shape?

It's a triangle. Can you think of anything that's shaped like a triangle?

We used the triangle to help us think about Up, In and Out, but today we'll use it to think about God's love story. This triangle can help us to see what a friendship with God looks like.

God used Abraham to show people what it's like to be friends with him. The great news of the Bible is that any of us can have that special friendship with God, starting today.

Here's how it works:

FATHER

OBEDIENCE   IDENTITY

Father
At the top of the triangle is the word Father. That's because the number one thing we have to remember is that God wants to be our Dad in heaven. He's a perfect Dad!

Your dad might be pretty awesome, but God is the best Dad ever. Abraham learned that God always loves us, protects us, and gives us what we need.

Identity
That leads to the next part of the triangle. Identity. Identity means who you are. Remember how God gave Abraham a new name? He does the same for you. Because God is your Dad, you are a kid of the King! That means you are special to God no matter what good or bad things you do. It means you always have a place in God's family. Whatever you do, God loves you just the same.

Obedience
God's love for us doesn't stop there! It helps us to obey God. We don't obey God to make him like us more. We don't obey God to get into heaven. We obey God

just because we love him. Because we're kids of the King, we want to act like kids of the King. We want to do the things the King loves because we love him so much. Abraham obeyed God because he loved him and trusted him.

 LOOK UP! God wants to be your Dad in heaven. Tell him at least three things you love about him right now.

 LOOK IN! Since you're a kid of the King, how should you treat God's other kids? Do you make fun of other kids or use words that build them up? Are you selfish with your stuff, or kind and generous?

 LOOK OUT! God always wants his family to keep growing. He wants everybody to become a kid of the King. Who can you pray for today who doesn't know Jesus?

God, thanks for being the best Dad ever. Thanks that you love me no matter what I do. Please help me to live like a kid of the King. Amen.

It's All About Me

Read: Genesis 37:1-11

Remember: Apart from me you can do nothing.
— John 15:5b (NIV)

Have you ever met people who are stuck on themselves? All they talk about is their great accomplishments and what they like to do. You would think the whole world revolves around them. It's not very much fun to be around people like that, is it? Joseph's brothers sure didn't think so, either.

HAVE YOU EVER BEEN AROUND SOMEONE THAT ONLY TALKS ABOUT THEMSELVES?

Joseph was Abraham's great-grandson. He was the youngest of twelve brothers and his dad's favorite. His dad gave Joseph all the best presents and never made him do any work. You can imagine this made his brothers pretty mad.

Then God started giving Joseph some special dreams. In these dreams, God was telling Joseph about how someday He was going to use him to do big things. Someday, God would use Joseph to rule.

Instead of just keeping the dreams to himself, though, or sharing them with one or two people, Joseph made the mistake of bragging about the dreams to everyone. He told his brothers he had the coolest dream. In the dream, they were out in the field tying up bundles of grain, and all of his brothers' bundles started bowing down to Joseph's.

It was like Joseph was in charge of all of his brothers, which he thought was pretty awesome. His brothers did not agree. In fact, sharing these dreams made them hate Joseph even more. But Joseph was clueless because all he could think about was himself. He didn't think about how his words and actions hurt other people. Worst of all, he didn't realize how much he needed God.

Before God could do any big kingdom stuff through Joseph, He would have to teach Joseph how to depend on God. It's the same way with us. If we want to do big things with God, we have to learn that we can't do anything without God.

LOOK UP! Kids of the King put God first, not themselves. Make a list of ten things that are awesome about God.

LOOK IN! Kids of the King put others second, right after God. Practice letting your friends go first at home, at school, and in your neighborhood.

LOOK OUT! Kids of the King share God's love by serving others. Do a top-secret act of kindness this week. Find someone who doesn't know God and give them a gift or do something nice for them without letting them know it was you.

God, thank you for letting me be a part of the big things you're doing. Please help me to remember that without you, I can't do anything. Amen!

Mr. Unpopular

Read: Genesis 37:12-36

Remember: And we know that in all things God works for the good of those who love him, who have been called according to his purpose.
— Romans 8:28 (NIV)

Have you ever had a really bad day? I mean like the worst day ever? Joseph did. Everything was going great for him at first. His dad gave him a cool coat and let him sit around while his brothers did all the work. Plus, God was sending him these crazy dreams about how someday he would rule over his family.

All these things made Joseph's brothers hate him.

One day, Joseph's dad sent him out to the field to check up on his brothers to make sure they weren't goofing off. When they saw him coming, they knew it was their chance to get rid of Joseph once and for all. So they beat him up, tore off his awesome coat, and threw him in a pit.

Then, just when Joseph thought things couldn't get any worse, some traveling salesmen came by on their way to Egypt. Joseph's brothers decided to sell him to them as a slave. I don't know if your brothers or sisters have ever done mean things to you, but at least they've never sold you as a slave.

HAS ANYONE EVER DONE ANYTHING MEAN TO YOU?

The traveling salesmen took Joseph off to Egypt, a foreign country where he didn't have any friends. You'd think Joseph's dad would come looking for him, right? But the brothers lied to him and showed him Joseph's shredded coat. They made him think Joseph had been killed by a wild animal.

Just imagine that you're Joseph, beaten up by your brothers and working as a slave in a foreign country. You're all alone. Your brothers hate you, and your dad thinks you're dead. That is one bad day.

What Joseph didn't know at the time was that this wasn't the end of his story. It was just the beginning. This was all part of God's wonderful dreams for Joseph coming true. God wanted Joseph to go to Egypt. Egypt was where Joseph would someday get to do big things with God.

Joseph had no idea that this was all part of God's great plan. At first, all he could see were the bad things that were happening. When you're in the middle of a story, it's sometimes hard to see how it could have a happy ending.

When you have a bad day, remember that your Dad in heaven is also the King. You can always trust that the King has everything under control, and He has a great plan for your life.

LOOK UP!

Draw a picture of a king on a throne. Around him, draw some of the things that are hard for you right now. Use this picture to remind yourself that even though life can be hard, God is still in control.

LOOK IN!

Friends of God pray for each other and remind each other of God's goodness. Which of God's friends do you need to pray for today?

LOOK OUT!

People who are going through tough times need to see God's love in action. Who do you know who is going through something difficult? How can you show them that God cares about them even though life is hard right now?

God, you are the King of everything. Help me to trust you to work things out even when bad things are happening. Remind me that you have a great plan for my life. Amen!

The Secret to Success

Read: Genesis 39:1-5

Remember: The Lord was with Joseph. He gave him great success.
– Genesis 39:2 (NIrV)

Have you ever known someone who was really good at something? Maybe they were a super soccer player or a math whiz. Maybe they were good at building stuff or creating some kind of art. Whenever you saw them, you may have thought, "What is their secret? How did they get to be so good at that?"

The truth is that all of our talents and gifts come from God. He made our bodies and brains and gives each of us the ability to learn cool skills. Hard work and practice help us get better at the skills God gives us. This is true for everyone, even people who don't know God.

But when we're friends with God, He uses those same abilities in special ways that change the world. God can make cool things happen that we could never make happen on our own. That's how it was for Joseph.

After Joseph was sold as a slave, he was bought by a powerful man named Potiphar. Potiphar worked for Pharaoh, the king of Egypt. Potiphar was captain of Pharaoh's guard.

When Joseph went to work for him, something amazing happened. The Bible says, "The Lord gave him success in everything he did." (Genesis 39:3 NIV) In other words, everything Joseph touched was awesome. For every job Potiphar gave Joseph, he knocked it out of the park.

Potiphar thought, "Wow, this guy is good! Everything he does rocks!" So, Potiphar put Joseph in charge of his entire house. What was the secret to Joseph's success? It wasn't just talent and hard work. The Bible says, "The Lord was with Joseph so that he prospered." (Genesis 39:2 NIV)

Remember when God made that special promise to Abraham? He told Abraham that his family would become God's special people. Joseph was a part of that promise, too. After all, he was Abraham's great-grandson. God's covenant wasn't just for Abraham but for his whole family, including Joseph.

LOOK UP!

This week, look for the places where God helps you succeed in doing things you could never do on your own. Tell Him thanks and give God all the credit.

LOOK IN!

When you see other friends of God do something good, celebrate it! Encourage them to keep using their gifts to serve God and others.

LOOK OUT!

God gives us gifts and abilities to help others. Joseph's skills helped a whole country who didn't know God. How can you use your abilities to help someone who doesn't know God today?

God, thank you for giving me talents and abilities, and thanks for helping me use them in special ways for your kingdom. Amen!

What's His Name?

Read: Genesis 39:20-40:8

Remember: Turn all your worries over to him.
He cares about you.
– 1 Peter 5:7 (NIrV)

Have you ever felt left out or forgotten? Have you ever had friends invited to a party but you didn't get invited to go? Or have you ever had kids in your class go play without you and just leave you behind? Being left out stinks, doesn't it?

Joseph probably felt a little like this when he was waiting for God's dreams for him to come true.

Just when life was looking up for Joseph, some more bad things happened to him. He got thrown into jail for something he didn't even do. Now, he was not only a slave but also a slave in jail!

Around the same time, Pharaoh got mad at his royal butler and baker and threw them in jail with Joseph. One night, they had crazy dreams. With God's help, Joseph told the butler and the baker what the dreams meant. Guess what? The dreams came true.

One of the dreams meant that the butler would be set free from prison and get to go back to work for Pharaoh. This was surely good news for Joseph. The butler had major connections. He worked for the king of Egypt. You would think he would be so grateful that first thing he would do was get Joseph released.

However, the Bible says that once this guy got out, he forgot all about Joseph. In fact, it would be two more long years before the butler even gave Joseph another thought. Can you imagine how left out and forgotten Joseph must have felt?

HAVE YOU EVER FELT LEFT OUT?

However, even when Joseph was in prison, the Bible says that "the Lord was with him; he showed him kindness and granted him favor in the eyes of the prison warden." (Genesis 39:21 NIV) So the warden put Joseph in charge of everything in the jail.

God was teaching Joseph to depend on Him. Joseph didn't need the butler's help. He needed only God.

Even when everyone else had forgotten about Joseph, God did not forget him. God doesn't forget you, either. God was working out His plan for Joseph's life in a way that no one could see just like God is working out a great plan for your life, too.

LOOK UP! When you feel forgotten or overlooked, be honest with God. Tell Him about it. Ask Him to remind you that He's always with you.

LOOK IN! Do you have any friends of God who you've neglected lately? Any friends you've been too busy to spend time with? Make time for them this week.

LOOK OUT! Write an encouraging letter to someone this week who might feel forgotten. Remind them that you still care about them and God does, too.

God, thank you for never forgetting about me. Help me to trust you when I feel left out or alone. Amen.

Joseph's Big Break

Read: Genesis 41:1-16

Remember: I cannot do it, Joseph replied to Pharaoh, but God will give Pharaoh the answer he desires.
— Genesis 41:16

By the time we meet Joseph again, he is thirty years old. That means he's been a slave or a prisoner for thirteen years, almost half of his life. After all this time, how could God's dreams for Joseph ever come true?

The answer? Only through God. God was Joseph's only hope. Joseph knew he couldn't count on his talent or good looks or luck or anything else. The only one who could rescue him from prison and slavery was God.

Once Joseph figured that out, he was finally in a place where God could use him. So, one night, in the palace of Pharaoh, king of Egypt, God put His plan in motion. He sent Pharaoh a crazy dream about a bunch of skinny cows eating a bunch of fat cows and another dream about some thin stalks of wheat eating some healthy stalks of wheat.

Weird, right? Pharaoh thought so, too. He woke up totally freaked out because he knew these were special dreams that had a hidden meaning. He called all of his wise men together, but no one could tell him what the dreams meant.

Then his butler spoke up and said, "Hey, remember when you got mad at me and threw me in jail? There was a guy there who told me what my dreams meant, and everything he said came true."

"What are you waiting for?" Pharaoh said. "Get him over here!"

So they cleaned Joseph up and brought him before Pharaoh. Finally, his big moment had arrived. Here he was standing in front of the most powerful man in the world. If Joseph could impress Pharaoh, maybe Pharaoh would set him free or even give him a reward.

Pharaoh said to Joseph, "I had a dream. No one can tell me what it means. But I've heard that when you hear a dream you can explain it.'" – Genesis 41:15 (NIrV)

Joseph could have tried to show off by telling Pharaoh about the dreams he had had when he was a kid. He could have bragged about being a dream expert. But Joseph didn't do any of those things.

He simply said, "I cannot do it . . . BUT God will give Pharaoh the answer he wants." (Genesis 41:16.NIrV)

Wow, can you believe that? Joseph didn't try to take any credit. He didn't try to show off. In fact, he said he couldn't even do the job. Only God could.

As a slave and a prisoner, Joseph had learned what it meant to be humble. When he was young, he had thought the world was all about him, but now he knew it was all about God. Joseph told Pharaoh the meaning of the dreams, and Pharaoh was so impressed he made Joseph second-in-command of all of Egypt.

God's dreams for Joseph had finally come true.

LOOK UP!
Every time you're tempted to brag about yourself this week, practice bragging about God instead. Tell people the cool things God has done in your life and for others.

LOOK IN!
Friends of God brag about other people, not themselves. Who is one friend you can brag about today?

LOOK OUT!
One way we can share God's love is by celebrating people the rest of the world overlooks. Have your family throw a surprise party for someone who never gets celebrated.

God, you are awesome. You can do anything. Please help me to remember that life is all about you, God. Give me the chance to brag about you this week. Amen!

Moving On Up

Read: Genesis 41: 41-57

Remember: Don't be like that. Instead, anyone who wants to be important among you must be your servant.
– Matthew 20:26 (NIrV)

Have you ever met someone who likes to boss people around? Some people always want to be the leader so they can give orders. They love having everything their own way.

God doesn't put us in charge of things to be bossy or selfish. He puts us in charge of things to do good. He makes us leaders over people and things to bring the good stuff from heaven to earth.

God's dream for Joseph had finally come true. He was second-in-command to the most powerful ruler on earth, but God had put Joseph there to help people. Joseph now had a big job to do.

Pharaoh's dreams were a special message from God. Through the dreams, God said that for the next seven years Egypt would have a whole lot of food. The crops would grow great, and everyone would have plenty to eat. However, for seven years after that, there would be a terrible famine. The crops would die. People would starve.

Joseph used his God-given wisdom to come up with a plan. During the years when they would have plenty of food, Joseph had the people store extra food in every city in Egypt.

Then, when the famine came, everyone in Egypt would have food to eat. In fact, people came from all over the world to buy food because the famine was so bad. Joseph's plan saved the lives of thousands of people.

God gives us authority and power to help others. If you get to lead something for your teacher at school, become the captain of a sports team, or even if you're just in charge of your little brother for the day, use it as a chance to do good.

LOOK UP! God is the biggest King ever, yet He serves us and helps us all the time. Make a list of ten things God has done for you.

LOOK IN! Are you bossy with your friends? Do you always have to pick the game to play or the movie to watch? If that's you, ask your friends what they want to do or watch instead. See how many times you can put others first this week.

LOOK OUT! Where are you a leader? With a baby brother or sister? On the playground at school? On a sports team? How can you serve the people you lead this week?

God, thank you for the chance to lead. Please help me to see how I can bring the good stuff from heaven to earth this week. Amen!

Helping Others Figure it Out

Read: Genesis 41: 1-8

Remember: The way of fools seems right to them, but the wise listen to advice.
— Proverbs 12:15

Do you remember what this shape is? It's a circle. What do you see around you right now that's shaped like a circle?

Like we talked about before, the circle reminds us how we can hear from God and do what he says. That's something we all need help with. That's why God gives us faith-filled friends to help us figure out what God's saying and what we need to do about it.

Take Pharaoh, for example. He didn't even know God, but God gave him some special dreams as a warning to save his people. But Pharaoh had no idea what the dreams meant or what he was supposed to do about them.

HAVE YOU EVER NEEDED HELP FIGURING SOMETHING OUT?

That's where Joseph came in. God told Joseph what the dreams meant. He even told him what Pharaoh needed to do about it. God used Joseph to put Pharaoh's dreams into action.

We may not all have special dreams, but God talks to us in all kinds of ways every day. That's why we need people like Joseph in our lives, friends who know God and can help us to figure out what God is saying to us and what we need to do about it.

$$y + x \left(\frac{2}{3}\right) + z = @$$

$$\frac{2}{5} \times b + a \mid 3^2 =$$

?

LOOK UP! Do you know how to hear God's voice? Is it clear for you like it was for Joseph, or confusing like it was for Pharaoh?

LOOK IN! Who are some people in your life who love God? Who can help you figure out what God is saying to you? Who can help you put it into action? Maybe it's your mom or dad? Maybe it's a grandparent or older sibling or a teacher or a friend? Who can be like Joseph for you?

LOOK OUT! Pharaoh didn't know God, but God sure was trying to get Pharaoh's attention. Maybe you can be like Joseph and help someone else understand what God is saying to them.

God, thanks for talking to me. Please send me people who can help me to figure out what you're saying. Please use me to help others understand you better too. Amen.

The Ultimate Power

Read: Genesis 45:1-8

Remember: Forgive, just as the Lord forgave you.
  – Colossians 3:13 (NIrV)

Have you ever wanted to get revenge on someone who was mean to you? If your brother hits you, the first thing you probably want to do is hit him back, right? If someone says something mean to you, you want to say something mean to them.

Imagine if you were made king or queen for a day, and you had the chance to get revenge on all of your enemies. What if for one day you had the power to pay back the kid who made fun of you in gym class or the teacher who yelled at you in front of all of your friends? What would you do?

That was exactly the choice Joseph had to make. God's dream for Joseph had come true. He was now the ruler over all of Egypt, second-in-command to Pharaoh himself. Joseph could pretty much do whatever he wanted.

Then one day, when there was a food shortage, guess who came to Egypt looking for food? Joseph's brothers! The same brothers who had beaten him up, thrown him in a pit, sold him as a slave, and told their father he was dead. Because of what they had done, Joseph hadn't seen his home or his dad for more than thirteen years.

Now, here they were in Egypt looking for food, and Joseph was the guy in charge of all the food. When they met him, they had no idea who he even was. What would Joseph do?

Would he have soldiers beat them up, throw them in a pit, and make them slaves? Would he throw them in the jail he had been in for all of those years? Would he laugh at them and tell them that's what they get for being so mean?

WHAT WOULD YOU DO IF YOU WERE JOSEPH?

Or would he do something worse? Would he have them killed? He could have done any of those things. But he didn't.

Joseph wasn't ruling for himself. He was ruling for God. Joseph was leading in God's kingdom. In God's kingdom, the ultimate power isn't about getting revenge. The ultimate power comes when you choose to forgive.

So, Joseph forgave his brothers and brought his whole family, including his dad, to live with him in Egypt where he could take good care of them. By forgiving his brothers, Joseph undid the evil they had done to him. His act of mercy made their family whole again.

LOOK UP!

Think about how much God loves you, even though you've done wrong things. Tell Him thank you for His forgiveness today.

LOOK IN!

Write down a way someone has hurt you. Pray about it and choose to forgive them like God forgives you. Tear up the paper and let it go.

LOOK OUT!

Forgiving our enemies is one of the most powerful ways to show the world that God is real. Has someone who doesn't know God hurt your feelings or been mean to you? Choose to forgive them and not get revenge.

God, thank you for forgiving me through Jesus. I want to do things your way. Please help me to be like Jesus and forgive others. Amen.

God's Adventure Story

We've seen this shape a few times before. What is it? Do you see any triangles around you right now? We've already used the triangle several times before, but today we're going to use it to talk about God's adventure story.

Joseph's life reminds us that God doesn't just want us to be His kids. He also has big, exciting work for us to do. We are kids of the King, but the King is on an adventure, and we get to join Him.

This triangle will help you understand what it looks like to do big things with God, like Joseph did.

Check it out:

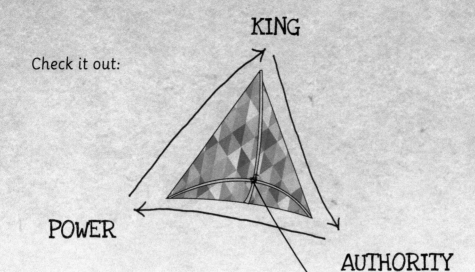

King

Since this is God's adventure, the triangle starts with God. It starts by understanding that's God's not just our Dad; He's also the King of the universe. In Joseph's story, he learned that he wasn't the center of the universe. The King is. Once Joseph gave up his pride, God could use him to do something awesome.

Authority

Because we're kids of the King, we have the authority to act for the King. We have permission from the King to do His work. As God's kids, we can take action for God. God gave Joseph the authority to step up and save the day when the famine came. He gives us royal authority to do good stuff, too.

Power

The King not only gives us permission to do His work but also gives us the power to make it happen. Joseph had the authority to act for God, but God also gave Joseph the power to save everyone from the food shortage. He gave Joseph the ability to figure out what Pharaoh's dreams meant. He also made Joseph really good at leading the people to save all the food and store it away.

Who would have guessed that Joseph would end up saving the world? But when we follow the King, there's no telling what adventures He has in store.

LOOK UP! Praise God for being an awesome King. Spend some time today thinking about how big and powerful He is.

LOOK IN! Who are one or two friends you can include in your adventure? Start praying today for God to send you other kids of King to join you on your mission.

LOOK OUT! Where do you think the King wants you to do some good with His authority and power this week? Who can you help? Where can you bring God's kingdom to earth?

God, you are an amazing King. You are bigger and stronger than I can even imagine. Thank you for inviting me to join your adventure today. Amen!

Help!

Read: Exodus 1:6-22

Remember: I love the LORD, for he heard my
voice; he heard my cry for mercy.
— Psalm 116:1 (NIV)

For a while, it looked like Joseph's family would live happily ever after in Egypt. Then Joseph grew old and died, and a new Pharaoh came to power. He didn't know about Joseph or how Joseph had saved the Egyptians.

Joseph's family had kids, and then their kids had kids and their kids had kids, until they were all over Egypt and became very powerful. This scared the new Pharaoh. He was afraid the Israelites would someday fight his people.

So he made the Israelites his slaves, and forced them to work hard all the time.

But wait, it gets worse!

Every time an Israelite boy was born, Pharaoh's soldiers would throw the baby into the Nile River so he wouldn't grow up to fight against the Egyptians.

The Israelites didn't know what to do. They could never escape Egypt on their own so they cried out to God for help . . . and God heard their prayers.

He sent them a new hero, a man named Moses.

God is the best covenant friend ever and the best Dad ever. God loves to help His kids!

LOOK UP! God is your Dad in heaven. He hears your prayers. Do you ask Him for help? Talk to your Dad in heaven today about what you need.

LOOK IN! Kids of the King pray for the needs of God's family. Which of your Christian friends do you need to pray for today?

LOOK OUT! One way you can show God's love is by praying for the needs of others who don't know God. Who do you know outside God's family who needs prayer today?

God, thank you for listening to my prayers. Thank you for helping me. Please remind me that I can always ask you for help. Amen!

No Ordinary Baby

Read: Exodus 2:1-15

Remember: For we are God's handiwork,
created in Christ Jesus to do
good works, which God prepared in
advance for us to do.
– Ephesians 2:10 (NIV)

Have you ever felt kind of ordinary? Well, the good news is that God loves using ordinary people to do extraordinary things. Take Moses, for instance. He was born to an ordinary Israelite woman in Egypt just like other babies.

Even when Moses was a baby, though, God was preparing him to do extraordinary things.

When Moses was three months old, his mom hid him in a tiny boat she had made from a basket. She put him in the tall reeds in the river to save him from Pharaoh.

You'll never guess who found him in the river. Pharaoh's own daughter! The princess! This was all part of God's plan. She felt sorry for Moses and took him home to raise as her own child.

Moses grew up as royalty in Pharaoh's palace. That meant he got a royal education and learned all kinds of things about Egypt. God was preparing ordinary Moses for a big job just like He had prepared Joseph many years before.

When Moses had grown up, he could have just kicked back and enjoyed being a prince of Egypt. But he didn't. He saw how cruel the Egyptians were to his people. He knew God had made him to do something about it.

However, Moses didn't wait for God's plan. He tried to do things his own way and totally messed it up.

DO YOU EVER FIND IT HARD TO WAIT?

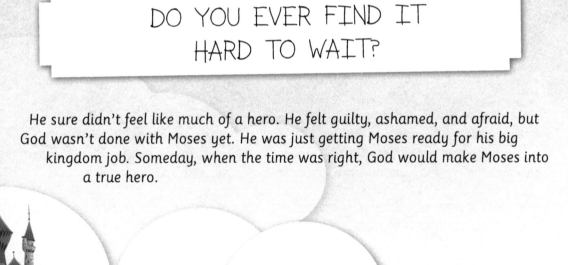

He sure didn't feel like much of a hero. He felt guilty, ashamed, and afraid, but God wasn't done with Moses yet. He was just getting Moses ready for his big kingdom job. Someday, when the time was right, God would make Moses into a true hero.

Sometimes when we try to do good things, we may mess them up, too. We may try to help someone and just make the situation worse. We may feel like we're ordinary people who can do only ordinary things.

That's when we need to remember that God's our Dad, and that makes us kids of the King. Even though we may feel ordinary, even though we may make mistakes, we've been made to change the world. God will give us all the wisdom and power we need to do big things with Him.

LOOK UP!

You may feel ordinary, but God made you to do big things in His kingdom. God's love and power make you special.

LOOK IN!

Doing what's right can be tough. That why we need to encourage our friends to not give up trying to do good even when they make mistakes. Which of your friends needs some encouragement today?

LOOK OUT!

Doing big things with God can start with little things. Small acts of kindness can change a person's life. What is one little thing you can do today to show kindness to someone who doesn't know God?

God, thank you for making me special. Please help me to remember that I can do big things with you. Amen!

CPSIA information can be obtained
at www.ICGtesting.com
Printed in the USA
LVHW072151091121
702921LV00023B/518